Two Lists for Christmas

Written by Lisa Pieterse-Carson

Illustrated by Ethan Roffler

Dedicated to my best friend Nicole (Coco) Mousseau

~ Thank You ~

A. Pieterse, M. Carson, E. Gould, L. Boffa, C. Lindeman, L. Hayse and J. Burns

Published by Doing Stuff Creative LLC
Copyright © 2020
ISBN: 978-1-7373892-0-0

Illustrations and layout by Stories Untold LLC

The little cabin was filled with commotion as the six friends put the final touches on their annual Christmas Wish-List Party.

Decorating duties were almost complete as Eunice Unicorn finished the tree. Lulu Llama hung everyone's stockings by the fireplace and Ozzy Octopus tied the last string of lights.

On the other side of the room, Millie Monkey placed paper and pens on the table. Sammy Sloth poured cups of hot cocoa and Dragon brought out his homemade cookies. This was going to be the BEST Christmas Wish-List Party ever!

Once everything was set, the six friends gathered around the table to enjoy their tasty treats and start writing their Christmas Wish-Lists. Each one talked about the presents they wanted Santa to bring them. They wanted TOYS - GAMES - GADGETS - BOOKS - BIKES - and MORE!

Their Christmas Wish-Lists went ON ... and OOON... and OOOOOOON... when suddenly...

A huge CRASH came from the rooftop...followed by a BUMP – then a BANG – then a BOOM and finally, an enormous THUD outside the window. Everyone ran outside to see what the racket was all about.

Their eyes widened... Santa? Reindeer? A sleigh?
But it wasn't even Christmas yet!

Reindeer reins were tangled up in a tree. Santa's sleigh was flipped upside down, and presents were scattered *EVERYWHERE*. The reindeer looked a little dizzy from the fall, and Santa was scratching his head trying to figure out what went wrong.

"THAT was a doozy!" Santa exclaimed. "I think we came in a little too fast with too many presents in tow. We completely missed the roof! Is everyone OK?"

"We're all good!" shouted Dasher. "But we might need to take a little break before heading out again."

"Ahem." Dragon cleared his throat. "I beg your pardon, Santa, but would you and the reindeer care to come inside and rest for a moment?"

"We have cookies and cocoa," added Ozzy enthusiastically.

"That sounds like a marvelous idea," said Santa.

"Santa, what are all of you doing out before Christmas Eve?" asked Eunice.

"A practice run," said Santa. "We train all year round for Christmas. Just like anything you want to be good at, it takes practice." Then Santa looked around the yard and asked himself. "How am I ever going to fix all of this?"

Ozzy Octopus pulled his friends together. "Why don't WE help Santa and his reindeer?"

"That sounds wonderful!" gushed Lulu Llama.

"I'll give it a go!" said Dragon.

The rest of the group was not so sure.
"I have more in common with rainbows than sleighs," said Eunice Unicorn with her hooves on her hips.

"I'm faaar toooo slow to assist," said Sammy Sloth as he looked down at the ground.

"And I'm simply too small to help those big reindeer," explained Millie Monkey.

"Well, we won't know what we can do or what we are good at until we give it a try," Ozzy Octopus said. "So, are we ready to do this?"

"Yes!" exclaimed Lulu and Dragon in unison.
The rest of the group still looked doubtful, so Ozzy tried a few words of encouragement. "I know this is something we have never done before, but Santa really needs our help." He smiled at his friends and added, "If we work together, I know we can figure it out. Come on!"
And everyone agreed to give it a try.

"Ugh, what a HUMONGOUS mess!" said Eunice Unicorn. "Where do you think we should start, Millie?"

Millie monkey looked confused. "Wh... Why are you asking me?"

"Because you're always coming up with neat ideas and creations," said Lulu.

Millie felt nervous. She took a deep breath and scurried around the lawn to take a closer look at the chaos.
After a few minutes, she returned with the plan.

Millie politely began assigning tasks to the group. She asked Lulu to supervise Santa and his reindeer inside and for Sammy to go to the roof and wait for her there. Millie then directed Eunice to untangle the reins from the tree with her horn, for Dragon to push the sleigh upright with his strong tail, and for Ozzy to collect all the presents with his many tentacles.

By the time everything was organized on the ground, Sammy had made it to the rooftop. Millie climbed up the side of the house to join Sammy and encouraged him to use his remarkable arm strength to pull the sleigh to the top of the cabin.

Back inside, Lulu Llama was tucking a blanket around one of the reindeer.

"Wow, Lulu, they look so cozy," said Ozzy Octopus.

Dragon nudged Santa awake to let him know that everything was ready to go.

"Wait." Santa paused for a moment. "Do you mean to tell me that the sleigh is untangled and on the roof?"

"It sure is," said Eunice Unicorn, and she shared the story of how everyone worked together to get the job done.

"Why, this is absolutely spectacular news! The reindeer and I thank you for everything you have done for us. It looks like we will be able to make it back to the North Pole to finish our training and be ready for the big day! Let's wake everyone up and we'll be on our way," said Santa. "Aaand one more cookie for the road," he added with a wink. "Farewell!"

On the front lawn, the friends said their goodbyes and wished Santa and the reindeer a safe journey home.

That evening, Dragon, Eunice Unicorn, Sammy Sloth, Lulu Llama, Ozzy Octopus and Millie Monkey talked about the amazing day they'd had. They were so very proud and excited about what they had done to help Santa and his reindeer.

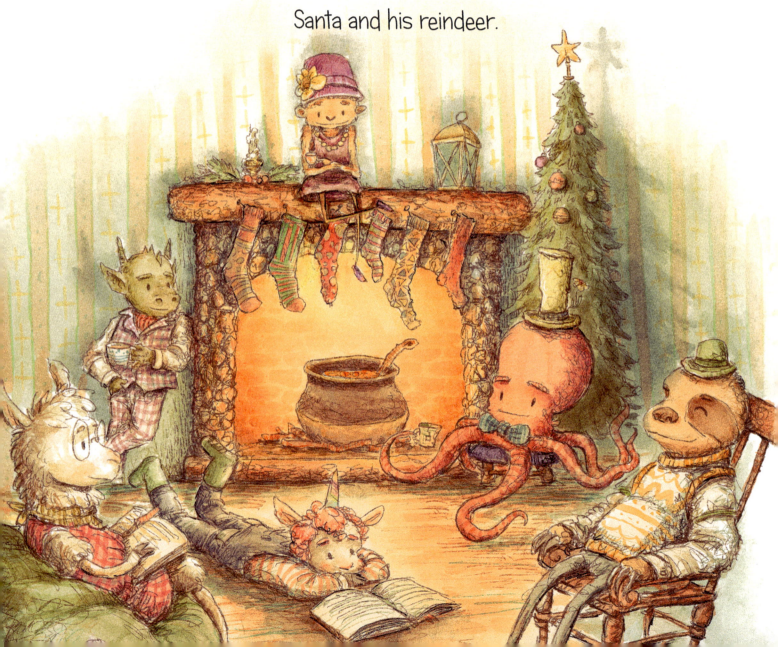

While they reminisced about the day's activities, the friends realized they had learned about a different kind of gift that day. It wasn't a toy or a game or a gadget. It didn't come in a box with a big bow from Santa. The *gift* was the amazing time they had while helping Santa. Working together and doing something nice for someone else made them all feel good and happy inside. It was called the *gift of giving*, and the friends learned how great it could feel to do something kind for someone else.

"I have an idea," said Lulu. "Why don't we make two Christmas lists?"

"Two lists?" asked Millie.

"Yes," said Lulu. "One list for Santa and one list of kind things we can do for others."

"And what sort of things could we put on this list?" asked Dragon.

"Let's see, what about saying something nice to someone?"
said Ozzy.

"What about picking up litter oooor holding the door open for someone?" said Sammy.

"Or donating toys that we don't use anymore!"
added Eunice.

"These are all great ideas for the new list!" said Lulu.

"Well, what should we call this list?" Eunice asked the group.

"Hmmmm...we already have the Christmas Wish-List that
we send Santa, what about ...
the Christmas Kindness-List?" suggested Sammy.
Everyone agreed.

Eunice Unicorn looked at her paper and began writing.

"Are you adding more to your Christmas Wish-List?" Lulu asked Eunice.

"Ummm...no. I'm taking a few things off it," said Eunice. "Even though I wanted it all, I realized that I don't really need it all. Plus, Santa and the reindeer already have so much to do and carry, this might help a little."
Eunice quickly adjusted her Christmas Wish-List, then excitedly started scribbling down ideas for her Christmas Kindness-List.

"Hmmm...I suppose I could shorten my wish list for Santa too," said Dragon, and he started crossing off items from his paper.

Everyone began doing the same, but they made sure to keep a few of their favorite wishes on their lists.

Sammy passed around the last of the cookies as the friends finished up their lists.

Then, Lulu Llama suggested, "From now on, let's always make two lists, one Christmas Wish-List for Santa and one Christmas Kindness-List for ourselves."

"It's a new Christmas tradition!" shouted Unicorn.

"This has been the best Christmas List Party ever!" said Ozzy. Everyone agreed.

The End

What would you put on your Christmas Kindness-List?

About the author

Having an eclectic background in entertainment and sport, Lisa spent several years working with children and young adults as a professional figure skating coach. During this time, she enjoyed sparking her student's creative side and encouraging them to step outside of their comfort zone to unearth abilities they did not know they had. These experiences inspired the development of her storybook characters, the way they approach new adventures and, in the end, learned life lessons.

Originally from Toronto Canada, Lisa currently resides in Southern Indiana with her husband Matthew and their dog Oya.

Made in the USA
Monee, IL
23 October 2021